D1142645

.NET Compact Framework
Pocket Guide

.NET Compact Framework
Pocket Guide

Wei-Meng Lee

Beijing · Cambridge · Farnham · Köln · Paris · Sebastopol · Taipei · Tokyo

.NET Compact Framework Pocket Guide
by Wei-Meng Lee

Copyright © 2004 O'Reilly Media, Inc. All rights reserved.
Printed in the United States of America.

Published by O'Reilly Media, Inc., 1005 Gravenstein Highway North,
Sebastopol, CA 95472.

O'Reilly & Associates books may be purchased for educational, business, or
sales promotional use. Online editions are also available for most titles
(*safari.oreilly.com*). For more information, contact our corporate/
institutional sales department: (800) 998-9938 or *corporate@oreilly.com*.

Editor:	Brian Jepson
Production Editor:	Marlowe Shaeffer
Cover Designer:	Emma Colby
Interior Designer:	David Futato

Printing History:

May 2004:	First Edition.

0-596-00757-4
[C]

Contents

Part III. Projects

Part IV. Deploying .NET Compact Framework Applications

.NET Compact Framework Pocket Guide

Introduction

The .NET Framework includes a runtime called the Common Language Runtime (CLR), compilers for languages such as C# and Visual Basic .NET, and the Framework Class Library (a large, factored class library that exposes many capabilities).

Browse the entries in the Class Library reference, and you'll find support for web services, networking, input and output, XML wrangling, and more. With all the capabilities in the .NET Framework, it's no surprise that the runtime weighs in as a 20 MB download (when it's extracted and installed, it's much larger than that). What's surprising, though, is how many capabilities are retained in the Microsoft® *.NET Compact Framework*, a scaled-down version of the .NET Framework for memory-constrained devices. In roughly 2.5 MB of file storage, and as little as 1.25 MB of runtime memory, you'll find support for core and extended .NET APIs, including collections, networking, ADO.NET data access, XML, and web services.

Conventions Used in This Book

The following typographical conventions are used in this book:

Italic
> Used to indicate new terms, URLs, filenames, file extensions, directories, commands and options, and program names. For example, a path in the filesystem will appear as *C:\windows\system*.

Constant width
> Used to show the contents of files or the output from commands.

Constant width bold
> Used in examples and tables to show commands or other text that should be typed literally by the user.

Constant width italic
> Used in examples and tables to show text that should be replaced with user-supplied values.

TIP

Indicates a tip, suggestion, or general note.

WARNING

Indicates a warning or caution.

For more information, visit O'Reilly's web site for this book, where examples, errata, and any plans for future editions are listed:

> *http://www.oreilly.com/catalog/compactframeworkpg*

Acknowledgments

I would like to thank Jonathan Wells, Product Manager of the .NET Compact Framework at Microsoft, for his support and review of this book. My editor Brian Jepson deserves a special mention for his attention to details and for making this book a better read. Thanks to Bill Takacs from O'Reilly, who made this book possible.

I would also like to thank Lori Piquet from DevX (a division of Jupitermedia Corp) who has kindly agreed to let me use some of my articles published at DevX.com for this Pocket Guide.

PART I

The .NET Framework and Mobile Devices

The .NET CLR

Runtimes like the CLR are called *managed execution environments* because they exert much more control over components than the operating system does. Although the operating system can usually guarantee that a rogue application won't bring the whole system down, modern applications are increasingly made up of cooperating components. The failure of a single component may not crash a modern operating system, but it can render an application unusable until the component is fixed. A managed environment like the CLR makes it easier to build reliable components by controlling component versioning, runtime execution, memory management, security, exception handling, and more.

Obtaining the .NET Compact Framework

The Microsoft® .NET Compact Framework is included with Visual Studio .NET 2003. You can deploy the .NET Compact Framework runtime directly to a supported device from within the Visual Studio .NET environment. The .NET Compact Framework is also built into any device based on Windows Mobile 2003.

Windows Powered Mobile Devices

There are several kinds of Mobile Devices that run a version of the Windows Mobile operating system, which is optimized for memory-constrained devices. The current incarnations of this operating system are descendants of the original Windows CE, and they include:

Pocket PC 2000/2002

This is a version of Windows that is designed for small devices with small screens (commonly 240 × 320 pixels) and no keyboard. Instead of a keyboard, there is a stylus and touch-sensitive screen, five-way navigation button, and a few buttons.

The previous version was Pocket PC 2000; many devices running the Pocket PC operating system can be upgraded to Pocket PC 2002. The .NET Compact Framework supports both Pocket PC 2000 and Pocket PC 2002 devices. Earlier versions of Windows CE, such as 2.11, are not supported by the .NET Compact Framework.

Pocket PC 2002 Phone Edition

This version of the Pocket PC 2002 operating system is for Pocket PCs with integrated phones. They still have the same screen, but they include support for voice telephony, SMS messaging, and General Packet Radio Service (GPRS) networking. Figure 1-1 shows the Pocket PC phone from T-Mobile. At the time of this writing, some carriers were rolling out upgrades that update Pocket PC 2002 phones to the Pocket PC 2003 Phone Edition (see "Windows CE .NET 4.2," later in this section).

Microsoft Smartphone

Microsoft Smartphones look less like a palm-sized computer and more like a phone. The navigation button is still there, along with a few buttons, but the Smartphone also has a telephone numeric keypad. The screen is smaller (for example, 176 × 220 pixels in the Motorola MPx200 Smartphone).

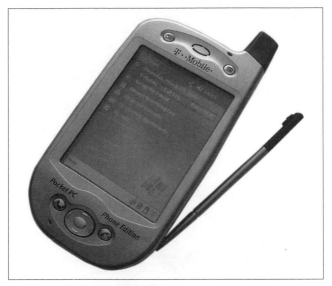

Figure 1-1. T-Mobile Pocket PC phone

Smartphones do not come with a stylus or touch-sensitive screen. Most devices in the market use the Smartphone 2002 operating system, although, at the time of writing, Smartphone 2003 was becoming available. The newer Smartphone 2003 operating systems come with the .NET Compact Framework (in the ROM), which allows applications to be developed using the .NET Compact Framework and the Smartphone 2003 SDK. Figure 1-2 shows the EverLink Wireless Smartphone, running the Smartphone 2003 operating system.

TIP

You must use Embedded Visual C++ to develop for the older Smartphone 2002 devices. Only the newer Smartphone 2003 devices support the .NET Compact Framework.

Figure 1-2. The EverLink Wireless Smartphone

Windows CE .NET 4.2/Windows Mobile 2003

Windows CE .NET is the latest version of the Windows CE operating system. It is the first of the Windows CE family to include the .NET Compact Framework (the runtime has to be installed separately for Pocket PC and Pocket PC 2002). Microsoft has also packaged this mobile operating system and branded it as Windows Mobile 2003 (commonly known as Pocket PC 2003), to better align its mobile platform with its Windows technology.

Most devices that you buy today use the Windows Mobile 2003 platform. Figure 1-3 shows the HP iPAQ 4150 Pocket PC.

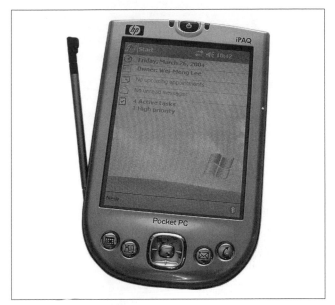

Figure 1-3. HP iPAQ 4150

If you are selecting a device to test .NET Compact Framework applications, check the version of the operating system against the previous list, and make sure the .NET Compact Framework supports it. Visual Studio .NET 2003 includes emulators for Windows CE .NET and Pocket PC 2002 so you can test .NET Compact Framework applications without needing to buy the hardware.

TIP

You must download the emulators for the Windows Mobile 2003 and Smartphone platforms separately from *http://msdn.microsoft.com/mobility/downloads/default.aspx*.

Networking

There are many ways that you can connect a mobile device to the network. You can use a network connection to transfer files between your development machine and the mobile device, or you can gain access to a network such as a corporate intranet or the Internet. Network access is critical for .NET Compact Framework applications that must connect to a web service or SQL Server database.

Although your .NET Compact Framework applications may need to connect to a network, the nature of wireless connectivity is such that you can't guarantee continuous access. The .NET Compact Framework was designed with this limitation in mind. For example, ADO.NET supports a disconnected data model: you can connect to the network when you need to obtain some data, modify it while you are offline, and synchronize when you get network access.

Tethered network access

If you don't mind being tethered to a desktop or laptop PC, you can use a Pocket PC cradle or ActiveSync cable. As soon as you activate the ActiveSync software, the mobile device will gain access to the network that your PC is connected to. This is accomplished through the same infrastructure used by Windows' Remote Access Service (RAS). The ActiveSync connection is also used by Visual Studio .NET to deploy applications directly to a mobile device.

Short-range wireless network access

If you don't want to be tethered to a PC, you can use wireless networking to connect your device to your PC or a wireless access point using Bluetooth or Wi-Fi:

- Bluetooth is a short-range, low-power wireless cable replacement. If you have a Bluetooth-enabled mobile device and a Bluetooth-enabled PC, you can use Active-Sync over Bluetooth. Some Bluetooth adapters include software to allow your PC to act as a LAN access point, and you can connect your mobile device to it as though it were a wireless router (there are also dedicated Bluetooth LAN access points that you can attach to your network).

- Wi-Fi is a medium-range wired LAN replacement that's also known by more technical names: 802.11b, 802.11a, and 802.11g. 802.11b was the first widely available wireless networking technology, originally introduced by Apple under the name AirPort. It operates at speeds of up to 11 Mbps; 802.11a and 802.11g can run as fast as 54 Mbps.

Bluetooth and Wi-Fi are built into some Pocket PC models, and adapters are available from many networking equipment manufacturers. Bluetooth has a typical range of 10 meters. Wi-Fi has a range of between 50 and 100 meters, but its range can be extended dramatically (up to 50 miles have been reported with the right equipment and a clear line of sight).

Long-range wireless network access

If you have a highly mobile workforce, you may not be able to keep your users within 100 meters of your corporate network. If your users spend a lot of time in airports, convention centers, and coffee shops, they may be able to take advantage of Wi-Fi hotspots, such as those offered by T-Mobile (*http://www.t-mobile.com*), Boingo (*http://www.boingo.com*), WayPort (*http://www.wayport.com*), and others.

If Wi-Fi hotspots are not sufficient for your needs, you may need to look at cellular networking protocols, such as General Packet Radio Service (GPRS) and Code Division Multiple Access (CDMA):

GPRS
> This is a slow (up to 40 Kbps) cellular protocol, but it is cheap (T-Mobile USA offers unlimited GPRS for as little as $20 a month).

CDMA 1x

This protocol is considerably faster than GPRS. The most widely deployed 1x technology is 1xRTT (1x Radio Transmission Technology), with speeds of around 50–70 Kbps, bursting to 144 Kbps). 1xEV-DO (1x Evolution Data Only) is an emerging 1x technology that is being rolled out in the U.S. and other places. It offers speeds of around 300–500 Kbps, bursting up to 2.4 Mbps.

Unlimited data plans for both GPRS and CDMA are available for around $80 a month, with the exception of T-Mobile USA, which offers unlimited GPRS for $20 (as an add-on to most voice plans) or $30 (as a standalone plan) per month. For other providers, cheaper plans are typically available in blocks of data (for example, AT&T offers 8 MB of data per month for $20). AT&T Wireless and Cingular have both rolled out EDGE, an enhancement over GPRS that can achieve speeds of up to 230 Kbps. EDGE pricing is similar to that of GPRS.

To connect a mobile device to a cellular network, you will need to find a cellular modem that fits your device, or purchase a device with cellular networking built-in. Pocket PC Phones and Smartphones have built-in GPRS or CDMA capability. Some GPRS-capable phones also have Bluetooth; you can use a Bluetooth connection to turn your cellular phone into a modem with no cables at all. Figure 1-4 shows this configuration.

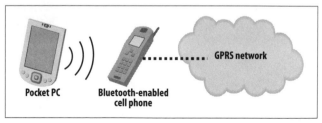

Figure 1-4. Connecting to the Internet through a Bluetooth-enabled cell phone

Tool and Language Support

To develop for the .NET Compact Framework, you'll need Visual Studio .NET 2003 or later. It includes the Visual Studio Integrated Development Environment (IDE), a Pocket PC Emulator, and the Smart Device Programmability features that let you develop and debug .NET Compact Framework applications. Visual Studio .NET 2003 provides two modes for testing your Smart Device Application: using either an emulator or a real device.

Visual Studio .NET lets you create .NET Compact Framework applications in C# or Visual Basic .NET. In the rest of Part I, we'll look at the Visual Studio .NET IDE and the building blocks of a simple .NET Compact Framework application.

TIP

In Visual Studio .NET 2003, .NET Compact Framework applications are known as *Smart Device Applications*.

Emulators

The easiest way to develop and test a Smart Device Application is to use an emulator. Visual Studio .NET 2003 provides two emulators—one to emulate the Windows CE .NET platform and one to emulate the Pocket PC 2002 platform. According to the product documentation, each emulator takes up an additional 64 MB of RAM. Our experience tells us that you need a moderately fast CPU with lots of memory. Our suggested memory requirement is 256 MB of RAM. Of course, if you have 512 MB or 1 GB of RAM, that will speed up the development and testing process.

The emulators provided by Visual Studio .NET are actual implementations of the Pocket PC (or Windows CE .NET) operating system that run on the x86 platform. This is different than a simulator, which is usually a Windows application that simulates the behavior of a device right down to emulating the underlying processor.

For hardware emulation, the emulators support two serial ports and one parallel port, which you can map to those on your development machine.

Device

For applications that make use of specific hardware features of the mobile device (such as Bluetooth), it is best to test your application on a real device. Visual Studio .NET 2003 allows you to test and debug your applications on a real device. This requires a connection between your computer and the device (via a USB or serial cable). You would also need Microsoft ActiveSync 3.7 (or later) so that the applications can be copied onto the device for testing.

The debugger in Visual Studio .NET 2003 allows you to step through your code, even though your application is deployed on the device. This is very helpful, as it allows you to debug your application in real time.

Testing your application on real devices often lets you discover performance problems that are not obvious when using an emulator.

Supported Languages and Platforms

The current release of the .NET Compact Framework in Visual Studio .NET 2003 supports only the Visual Basic .NET and C# languages. While the .NET Framework supports more than 30 languages, you are limited to these two languages in the .NET Compact Framework.

For the initial release of the .NET Compact Framework, Smart Device Applications can execute on the following platforms:

- Pocket PC 2000
- Pocket PC 2002
- Pocket PC 2002 Phone Edition
- Windows Mobile 2003 software for Pocket PC
- Windows Mobile 2003 software for Pocket PC Phone Edition
- Windows Mobile 2003 software for Smartphone
- Windows CE .NET 4.1 and later

While Pocket PC and Pocket PC 2002 are all based on the Windows CE 3.0 operating systems, the .NET Compact Framework will not run on devices with other operating systems based on Windows CE Version 3.0 or earlier, such as the Handheld PC 2000.

For developing applications on the Smartphone platform, you need to install the Smartphone 2003 SDK, a separate download available from *http://msdn.microsoft.com/mobility/ downloads/sdks/default.aspx*.

Hello, Pocket PC

To create a Smart Device Application, launch Visual Studio .NET 2003 and create a new project by clicking File → New Project. This first project uses Visual Basic .NET.

Select the desired language (in this case, Visual Basic .NET) under Project Types, and then select Smart Device Application under Templates (see Figure 1-5). Click the OK button.

You will be prompted to choose a target platform for your application: Pocket PC or Windows CE. In addition, there are five project types available:

Windows Application
    For developing applications with Graphical User Interface (GUI) features.

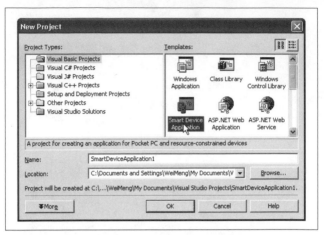

Figure 1-5. Developing a new Smart Device Application

Class Library

For developing class libraries that will be used in a Smart Device Application.

Non-graphical Application

For creating applications that do not need a user interface. It is usually for applications that run in the background.

Console Application

For creating an application that runs within the Windows CE .NET console. This option is applicable only to the Windows CE .NET platform. Choosing Windows CE as the platform will offer the Console Application project type instead of the Non-graphical Application.

Empty Project

For creating a new project that does not contain any files.

For our example, we will create a Windows Application for the Pocket PC platform. Click OK to complete the wizard (see Figure 1-6).

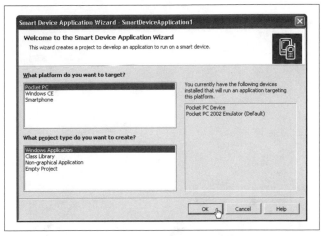

Figure 1-6. Choosing the platform and project type

Windows Mobile 2003 and Smartphone Support

Microsoft Visual Studio .NET 2003 ships with support of the .NET Compact Framework for Pocket PC and Pocket PC 2002 devices only. To develop for Windows Mobile 2003 devices and Smartphones, you need to download:

- Software Development Kit for Windows Mobile 2003-based Pocket PCs and Software Development Kit for Windows Mobile 2003-based Pocket PC Emulator Images
- Software Development Kit for Windows Mobile 2003-based Smartphones

Both SDKs are available for free download at *http://msdn. microsoft.com/mobile*.

You will now see Visual Studio .NET's IDE for developing .NET applications, as shown in Figure 1-7.

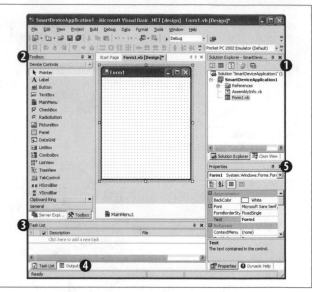

Figure 1-7. Using Visual Studio .NET 2003 for developing Smart Device Applications

Let's spend some time exploring the development environment.

Solution Explorer

The Solution Explorer displays the current projects and their various references and files. (You can display the Solution Explorer by clicking View → Solution Explorer.) In this example, the solution contains one Smart Device Application project (see Figure 1-7, callout ❶). Within this project are the various references to class libraries, as well as the forms in this project. It is often useful to have multiple projects in a solution so that you can debug multiple related projects without opening and closing project files.

If you want to add a new form to your project, you can right-click on the project name in Solution Explorer and select Add → Add New Item. The Add New Item dialog appears, which lets you specify the item type (for example, Windows Form). You don't need to do this because the Smart Device Application includes one form (Form1) by default.

If you have multiple forms in a project, Form1 will be loaded when the application is run. To change the startup form, right-click on the project name and select Properties. Change the Startup Object drop-down listbox to the form that you want to load when the application is loaded.

Toolbox

The Toolbox (Figure 1-7, callout ❷) contains the various controls that you can use in your Smart Device Application. By default, it is not fully visible. To make it appear, hover your mouse over the tab labeled Toolbox (which appears in the upper left of the Window). To make it disappear again, move the mouse off of the Toolbox. You can make the Toolbox permanently visible by clicking its pushpin control. You can turn it into a free-floating toolbar by dragging its titlebar.

We will examine the use of the various controls in more detail in Part II, which lists the controls available in the .NET Compact Framework.

Task List

The Task List window is usually located at the bottom of the screen (as shown in Figure 1-7, callout ❸). The Task List displays the list of errors (or warnings) in your code as you develop your application. You can make the Task List appear by selecting View → Other Windows → Task List.

Using the Task List window, you can see the list of errors and make corrections before you build and run your application.

Output

The Output window displays the messages generated during compilation time and runtime. The Output window is not shown in Figure 1-7, but its tab is visible at callout ❹; Figure 1-8 shows a free-floating version of this window. For example, if you try to build a Pocket PC application but fail due to some errors, the error message will be displayed on the Output window.

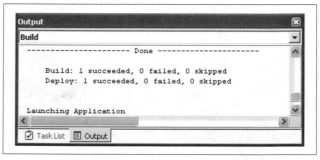

Figure 1-8. The Output window

In general, refer to the Output window when you encounter errors in running your application.

WARNING

The Console.Write( ) method is not supported in the .NET Compact Framework. Therefore, you cannot use it to write debugging information to the Output window.

Forms Designer

The Forms Designer is where you build the user interface of your application. To add a control to your Windows form, drag a control from the Toolbox and drop it onto the Windows form.

Properties Window

Use the Properties window (Figure 1-7, callout ❺) to change the appearance of a control (or form).

To display the Properties window for a control, right-click the control and select Properties. For example, to change the text of a Label, TextBox, or Button control from their default values, modify the Text property of each control. Figure 1-9 shows the appearance of the Label, TextBox, and Button controls after their default Text properties have been changed.

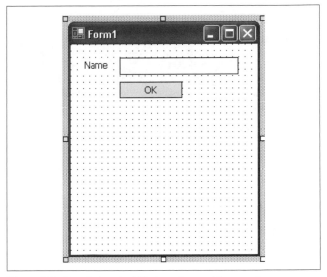

Figure 1-9. Populating the Windows form with controls

Code Window

To write code to "wire" up the controls, double-click the control that you want to program. This makes the Code window appear.

The Code window is where you write all your code for the application. As shown in Figure 1-10, Visual Studio .NET 2003 has generated all the relevant code for the various controls that you have dragged and dropped onto the Designer window.

```
Public Class Form1
    Inherits System.Windows.Forms.Form
    Friend WithEvents Label1 As System.Windows.Forms.Label
    Friend WithEvents TextBox1 As System.Windows.Forms.TextBox
    Friend WithEvents MainMenu1 As System.Windows.Forms.MainMenu

    Windows Form Designer generated code

    Private Sub Button1_Click(ByVal sender As System.Object, ByVal e As System.Even
        MsgBox("Hello, " + TextBox1.Text, _
            MsgBoxStyle.Exclamation, "Hello Pocket PC")
    End Sub
End Class
```

Figure 1-10. Switching to Code view

To wire up the OK button, simply add the following code to the Button1_Click method:

```
MsgBox("Hello, " + TextBox1.Text, _
    MsgBoxStyle.Exclamation, "Hello Pocket PC")
```

The Button1_Click method should now look like this:

```
Private Sub Button1_Click(ByVal sender As _
            System.Object, ByVal e As _
            System.EventArgs) Handles _
            Button1.Click
    MsgBox("Hello, " + TextBox1.Text, _
        MsgBoxStyle.Exclamation, "Hello Pocket PC")
End Sub
```

The line in the Button1_Click event handler displays a message box when the OK button is clicked.

Help

One of the survival skills that you need to possess as a .NET Developer is the ability to find help (or solutions) to your problems. The MSDN documentation that ships with Visual

---

Studio .NET 2003 is a gem—if you know how to make full use of it.

Apart from IntelliSense, which automatically displays a list of methods and properties relevant to an object when you press the "." after an object's name, there are other ways to get help in the event that you encounter a problem:

- Pressing F1 invokes the context-sensitive help. Context-sensitive help works both in the Design view as well as in the Code view. Simply select a control, or position your cursor at a particular method or property, and press F1.

- View the documentation for .NET Compact Framework by selecting Help → Contents from the menu.

- If you need to find a method or property quickly, you can use the Index located at Help → Index. You can set the filter to ".NET Compact Framework" so that only relevant information is presented to you.

- Finally, if you need to search for certain topics or keywords, use the search facility located at Help → Search.

Debugging the Application

The easiest and fastest way to test your application is to use the emulator. Visual Studio .NET ships with two emulators: Pocket PC 2002 for Pocket PC applications and Windows CE .NET for Windows CE applications (you can download others from *http://msdn.microsoft.com/mobility/downloads/sdks/default.aspx*). On the Device toolbar, you can choose to test your application using either an emulator or a real device (see Figure 1-11). Also, when you debug the application by pressing F5, you'll be prompted to choose one of the emulators, so you can make a selection from there.

The Pocket PC emulators emulate devices running the Pocket PC 2002 and Pocket PC 2003 platforms. Figure 1-12 shows the Pocket PC 2003 emulator.

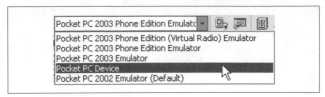

Figure 1-11. Test your application using an emulator or a real device

When you deploy your application for the first time on a given device or emulator, Visual Studio .NET copies all the relevant .NET Compact Framework assemblies to the emulator (except for the Pocket PC 2003 emulator, where the .NET Compact Framework is already present in the ROM), as shown in Figure 1-13.

It copies the executable of the current project to the device, and then copies and installs two CAB files onto the emulator (or device): *netcf.core.ppc3.x86.cab* and *System_SR_enu.cab*. You can verify the successful installation of these two CAB files by clicking Start → Settings → System → Remove Programs on your device. Figure 1-14 shows two components installed in the Pocket PC 2002 device versus the one component installed in a Windows Mobile 2003 device.

These programs take up a total of 1476 KB of memory (for Pocket PC 2002).

Testing the Application

After the application and the .NET Compact Framework have been deployed, Visual Studio .NET will launch the application on the emulator. Form1 should appear shortly. To test this application, enter a name in the text box and click the OK button. You should see a message box displaying a message, as shown in Figure 1-15.

That's it! This is your first Smart Device Application!

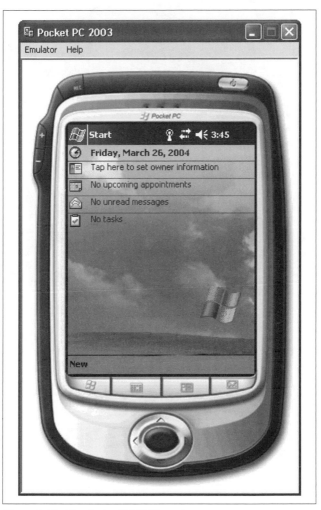

Figure 1-12. The Pocket PC 2003 emulator

Figure 1-13. Installing the .NET Compact Framework assemblies on the emulator

Figure 1-14. Verifying the successful installation of the .NET Compact Framework on a Pocket PC 2002 device and a Windows Mobile 2003 device

Figure 1-15. Testing the application on an emulator

Invoking the Emulators Manually

When you choose to run your Smart Device Application in Visual Studio .NET 2003 using the emulator, it will be automatically launched. However, there are times when you would want to launch the emulator without using Visual Studio .NET 2003. In that case, you can invoke the emulator manually, running it as a standalone application.

The emulator is located in the following directory (assuming *C:* is your system partition):

```
C:\Program Files\Microsoft Visual Studio .NET 2003\
CompactFrameworkSDK\ConnectionManager\Bin
```

The *emulator.exe* application supports the following options:

/Video
> Sets the resolution and bit-depth of the emulator for Windows CE display. Must be in *width × height × bit depth* format with width, height, and bit-depth as integers.

/Ethernet
> Enables or disables the Ethernet controller in the emulator for Windows CE. Uses values of none, shared, virtualswitch, or the MAC address of the Ethernet adapter.

/Skin
> Indicates which skin to use with the emulator for Windows CE. Requires an XML filename describing the skin.

/CEImage
> Indicates which Windows CE kernel image to use.

To launch the emulator for Pocket PC 2002, you can issue the following commands:

```
> cd C:\Program Files\Microsoft Visual Studio .NET 2003\
CompactFrameworkSDK\ConnectionManager\Bin
> start emulator /CEImage images\PocketPC\2002\1033\
PPC2002.bin /Video 240x320x16
```

For a Windows CE .NET Web pad emulator, use the following commands:

```
> cd C:\Program Files\Microsoft Visual Studio .NET 2003\
CompactFrameworkSDK\ConnectionManager\Bin
> start emulator /CEImage images\windowsce\webpad\1033\
wce4webpad.bin
```

TIP

We used the start command to invoke the emulator. Using the start command runs the emulator and immediately returns control to the command prompt.

Resetting the emulator

Resetting a real device is straightforward—most devices have a reset button located at the bottom of the device. But for emulators, you have two choices (these are available from the Emulator menu):

Soft reset
> Restarts the emulator. The emulator will retain all its previous settings.

Hard reset
> Restarts the emulator and restores the emulator to its original state. All programs that you have installed will be gone. In particular, the assemblies for the .NET Compact Framework will need to be reinstalled the next time you run your application from Visual Studio .NET 2003.

There are several reasons for resetting your emulator. We will cover some common problems later in the "Troubleshooting" section.

Deploying to a Mobile Device

The emulator is great for rapid code/compile/debug cycles, but nothing beats the real thing. So if you want to test your application on a real device, or deploy it to your mobile device so you can take your application on the road, simply change the device option in the Device toolbar to Pocket PC Device. You need to connect your Pocket PC to the computer beforehand using ActiveSync. Press F5 to compile and deploy the application, and it will launch on your mobile device.

To launch the program at a later time, on its own and not under the control of the Visual Studio .NET debugger, use the built-in File Explorer application to navigate to the directory that contains your application (such as *\My Device\ Program Files\SmartDeviceApplication1*), and tap on the application (such as *SmartDeviceApplication1*) to launch it.

WARNING

If you have an older version of the .NET Compact Framework installed, remove it from your device. Older versions of the framework will cause a deployment failure for your current project. You can uninstall the .NET Compact Framework by navigating to Start → Settings → System → Remove Programs.

The installation process is very similar to that of the emulator, with one notable exception. Instead of copying *netcf. core.ppc3.x86.cab*, it copies *netcf.core.platform.architecture. cab* (for example, on an iPAQ Pocket PC with an ARM processor, it would copy *netcf.core.ppc3.arm.cab*).

Troubleshooting

In the course of following the examples in this chapter, you may have encountered some problems in getting your Smart Device Application project to work. Here are some common errors that you may encounter and how to solve them:

Devices not connected

Typically, you will see this error message when you try to deploy your application to a real device. A common cause is that your device is not connected to the development machine via ActiveSync. The device might be connected physically, but check ActiveSync; if it states that the device is not connected, disconnect the device and try connecting again. You may need to reset the device or ensure that your USB (or serial) connection to the machine is working properly.

File sharing violations

This is another type of error that you may come across, especially if you have successfully run your application on either the emulator or device. Subsequent runs of the same application may display this message. This error occurs when the application on the emulator (or device) has, for some reason, failed to exit gracefully, and you have tried to run the application on it again (and Visual Studio .NET fails while copying over the file that is in use). In such cases, resetting the device will most likely solve the problem. For the emulator, try a soft reset first to see if the problem goes away; if it doesn't, use the hard reset. If everything fails, restart Visual Studio .NET and run your application again.

Missing network connection

You may not be able to launch your application if your computer does not have a network connection. If you do not have an active network connection, install the Microsoft Loopback adapter on your development machine. The Microsoft Loopback adapter is a virtual network device you can add using the Add/Remove Hardware control panel.

PART II

User Interface Design

Developing Pocket PC and Smartphone applications is similar to developing Windows applications; you lay out windows and controls and back them up with code. The number of Windows controls supported depends on the platform that you are targeting. For example, you can choose from 28 controls on the Pocket PC platform, while only 14 controls are available for the Smartphone. This part discusses the Windows controls available for each platform, as well as some design considerations for developing Windows Mobile applications.

Using the Windows Forms Controls

You can locate the controls in the Toolbox window (found on the left side of the Visual Studio .NET 2003 window; see Figure 2-1). If it is not visible, you can display the Toolbox window by pressing Ctrl-Alt-X or selecting Toolbox from the View menu.

Here are the controls supported by the .NET Compact Framework:

Label (Smartphone, Pocket PC)
Provides descriptive text.

Button (Pocket PC)
Allows the user to trigger an action by clicking.

Figure 2-1. Locating the Toolbox window

TextBox (Smartphone, Pocket PC)

Allows the user to enter textual information. This control accommodates multiple lines of text and supports horizontal and vertical scrollbars.

MainMenu (Smartphone, Pocket PC)

Represents a series of menu items.

CheckBox (Smartphone, Pocket PC)

Presents an option that can be toggled on and off.

RadioButton (Pocket PC)

Presents one or more mutually exclusive options.

PictureBox (Smartphone, Pocket PC)

Displays an image from a graphics file such as BMP, JPG, GIF, or PNG.

Panel (Smartphone, Pocket PC)

Contains other controls.

DataGrid (Smartphone, Pocket PC)

Binds to a data source, such as a dataset, and displays the records in a grid table.

ListBox (Pocket PC)

Displays a list of items from which the user can select. The ListBox control does not support multiple selections in the .NET Compact Framework.

ComboBox (Smartphone, Pocket PC)

Displays a list of items from which the user can select. It is similar to the ListBox, but includes an editing field so that users can enter text if the desired item cannot be found in the list.

ListView (Smartphone, Pocket PC)

Displays a list of items in various formats. You can also represent items as an icon in different sizes. Similar to the Windows Explorer file list view.

TreeView (Smartphone, Pocket PC)

Displays items in a hierarchical fashion. Similar to the Windows Explorer directory list.

TabControl (Pocket PC)

Contains TabPages, which allows multiple pages of information to be contained within a single form.

HScrollBar (Smartphone, Pocket PC)

Provides a horizontal scrollbar for controls that do not have scrollbar support.

VScrollBar (Smartphone, Pocket PC)

Provides a vertical scrollbar for controls that do not have scrollbar support.

Timer (Smartphone, Pocket PC)

Executes specified tasks, such as updating a progress bar, at a regular interval.

DomainUpDown (Pocket PC)

Contains two up and down buttons that allow users to select text from a predefined list. Users can also type text into the text field provided. Windows uses this in date/time choosers.

NumericUpDown (Pocket PC)

Contains a numeric value that users can increment or decrement by clicking on up and down buttons. It is similar to the DomainUpDown control, except it is restricted to numeric values. Windows uses this in date/time choosers.

TrackBar (Pocket PC)
>Behaves similarly to a scrollbar. You can set the value of the TrackBar during runtime and use it as a way to input values.

ProgressBar (Smartphone, Pocket PC)
>Displays a bar that is filled from left to right. It is often used as a visual feedback for a lengthy operation, such as accessing a web service.

ImageList (Smartphone, Pocket PC)
>Contains images used in conjunction with other controls, such as ListView, TreeView, and ToolBar.

ContextMenu (Pocket PC)
>Displays a context-sensitive menu when the user taps on a control and holds for a few seconds. Similar to the MainMenu control, except that it is not anchored at a particular spot.

ToolBar (Pocket PC)
>Displays a toolbar that provides shortcuts to commonly used tasks.

StatusBar (Pocket PC)
>Provides an area for displaying information, such as the status of the current operation. It is a useful control for providing feedback to the user.

OpenFileDialog (Pocket PC)
>Displays a common dialog window asking the user to open a file.

SaveFileDialog (Pocket PC)
>Asks the user to save a file; otherwise, it is similar to the OpenFileDialog control.

InputPanel (Pocket PC)
>Controls the Soft Input Panel (SIP) programmatically. The SIP displays either an on-screen keyboard or handwriting input region.

Part III shows some of these controls in action.

Design Considerations for Smartphone Applications

Despite the same development environment and the commonality of the .NET Compact Framework class libraries, developing for the Smartphone is not entirely the same as developing for the Pocket PC. Smartphone developers need to understand and appreciate the design constraints of the new platform. Part I shows some Windows Mobile 2003 devices.

One of the differences between a Smartphone and a device running the Pocket PC platform is its form-factor. Pocket PC devices use a stylus and a touch-sensitive screen for user input. Smartphones do not have touch-sensitive screens; instead, they depend on *softkeys* mapped to fixed buttons on the keypad, as well as a five-way navigation button. So instead of using Button controls, the user would click one of the two softkeys.

TIP

The form-factor for the Pocket PC Phone Edition is identical to the Pocket PC, so it also differs substantially from the Smartphone.

Figure 2-2 shows the typical layout of the navigational buttons on a Smartphone.

You scroll through the various controls on the screen using up/down clicks with the five-way navigation button; left and right are usually used for scrolling through options in controls, such as the ComboBox. An Action click (pressing in on the five-way navigation button) selects an option, somewhat equivalent to a "tap" in the Pocket PC.

Because there are only two softkeys, if you have more than two options, they need to be grouped together (see Figure 2-3). In this case, you'd name one of the two softkeys as Menu to let the user know that there are more than two options available.

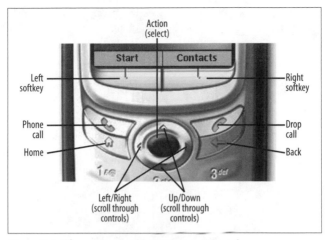

Figure 2-2. The navigational buttons on a Smartphone

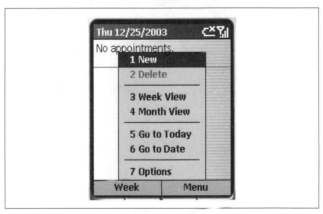

Figure 2-3. Grouping options together and assigning to a softkey

Screen Real Estate

A Pocket PC has a much larger screen than a Smartphone. A
Pocket PC screen size is typically 240 × 320 pixels, whereas

a Smartphone screen size is 176 × 180 pixels (minus the title and menu bar). Figure 2-4 shows a comparison in screen size between the two platforms.

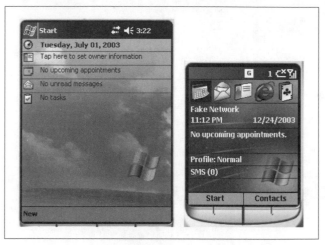

Figure 2-4. The Pocket PC's screen versus the Smartphone's

Drop-Down Menus

Because you can tap on the screen in a Pocket PC, the items in a drop-down menu drop downwards when clicked. In a Smartphone, however, there is no such control. To achieve the same effect, you need to customize the ListView control (see Figure 2-5). To select the item in this menu, you can use the up/down navigation action or press the shortcut key. For example, pressing "7" is equivalent to scrolling down to the MSN Messenger item and pressing the Action key.

User Input

The Pocket PC has a built-in SIP, but the Smartphone does not have one. Instead, the user has to rely on the numeric keypad to enter both text and numbers (see Figure 2-6).

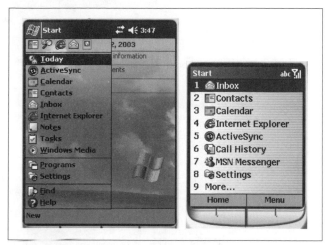

Figure 2-5. Implementations of the drop-down menu metaphor

When designing applications that require user input, be sure to minimize the number of keys the user has to press. Also, be sure to turn on numeric mode for fields that expect numbers (such as telephone numbers) and T9 input for alphanumeric fields.

If you turn on numeric mode for text input, the titlebar actually displays a "123" symbol to provide visual cues (see Figure 2-7). To change the input modes, simply press and hold the "*" key. The three modes—"123", "abc", and "t9"—will toggle.

Context Menus

Context menus are useful for displaying options related to a particular piece of information. However, context menus are not supported in the Smartphone. Instead, you have to make use of the softkeys to display menus related to a particular item (see Figure 2-8).

Figure 2-6. User input on the Pocket PC versus the Smartphone

Figure 2-7. Visual cues indicate the input mode

Text Input

For a single line of text input, the TextBox control on the Smartphone looks similar to that of the Pocket PC (see Figure 2-9).

For multiple lines of text input on the Smartphone, you will see a right arrow at the right end of the textbox. Press the

Figure 2-8. Context menus are not supported on the Smartphone

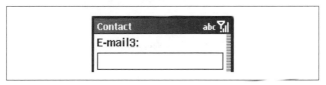

Figure 2-9. Single line text input

Action key to bring you to a full screen (Figure 2-10 shows the original view on the left, full screen view on the right).

ComboBox

For ComboBox controls, you will not see a drop-down list of items (as in the Pocket PC); instead, you will see two arrows at the right side of the text box. To scroll through the list of items, use the left/right navigation action. Alternatively, you can also press the Action key to view the list of items available for selection (Figure 2-11 shows the original view on the left, full screen view on the right).

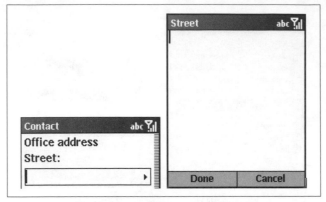

Figure 2-10. Multiple line text input

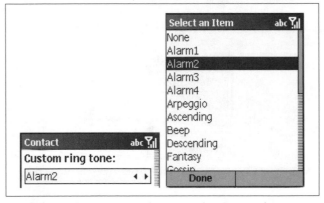

Figure 2-11. Selecting an item from a ComboBox control

Tab Control

In the Pocket PC, you use a Tab control when you have more controls than you have space to put them in (see Figure 2-12, left). However, the Smartphone does not support the Tab control.

When you have to display a large number of controls, there are two options available:

- Make the form scrollable to accommodate all the controls (see Figure 2-12, right).
- Use multiple Panel controls (to contain the other controls) and overlay them. Hide and display each Panel as the user walks through the application.

Figure 2-12. The Pocket PC's Tab control versus the Smartphone's scrolling forms

Projects

The best way to learn how to program using the .NET Compact Framework is to walk through some sample projects. This part shows you a number of projects that you can build using Visual Studio .NET 2003:

- Project A: Currency Converter
- Project B: Book Ordering System
- Project C: Bluetooth Chat

Project A: Currency Converter

This first project shows how to develop a simple currency converter using the .NET Compact Framework's built-in controls. For simplicity, the sample application is limited to three currencies: U.S. Dollar, CNY (Chinese Yuan), and Singapore Dollar. This application downloads the currency exchange rates from a web service when the application is first used. The application stores the rates in an XML document for subsequent usage.

Populating the Form with Controls

In Visual Studio .NET 2003, create a new Smart Device Application (File → New → Project, then select Visual Basic Projects → Smart Device Application). Set the Pocket PC as the target device and select a project type of Windows Application. Your project should open with the default Form1.

Before you can add any of the controls, you need to set up two tab forms.

The application in this project contains one TabControl control, which in turn contains two TabPage controls. The first tab page is called Conversion, while the second is called Set Rates. The TabPage control lets you spread the controls across two pages.

To set it up, drag the TabControl from the toolbox onto the form. To add the tab page to a TabControl control, select the TabControl, right-click on it, and select Add Tab (see Figure 3-1).

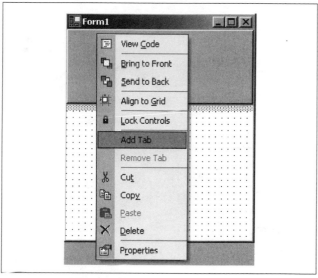

Figure 3-1. Add a new TabPage control

To change the label of the TabPage, click the tab, select the TabPage (the region just above the tab), right-click on it, and select Properties. Change the Text property of the TabPage to Conversion. Do the same for the second tab page, but set its text to Set Rates. You should enlarge the TabControl so that it fills the form.

You must add the controls listed in Table 3-1 to this form (see Figures 3-2 and 3-3 for the layout). You'll also need to add an Options item to the default MainMenu1.

Table 3-1. Controls used in the currency converter

Control type	Conversion tab	Set Rates tab
Label	lblResult	"Base Currency: US$", "Symbol", "Rate"
TextBox	txtValue	txtRate
ComboBox	ComboBox1, ComboBox2	ComboBox3
Button	cmd0–cmd9, cmdPt, cmdEq, cmdBackSpace, cmdClear	cmdUpdate
ListBox	ListBox1	

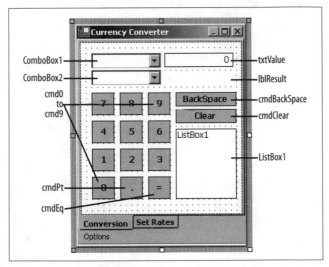

Figure 3-2. Setting up the form (Conversion tab page)

The first tab page (Conversion) contains two ComboBox controls for the user to select the currencies to convert. Once the currencies are selected, the user can click on the numbered Button controls to input the amount to convert. The

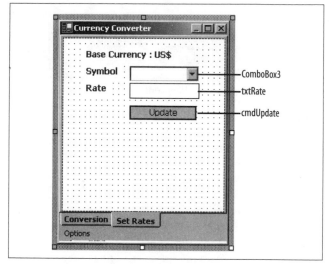

Figure 3-3. Setting up the form (Set Rates tab page)

BackSpace button deletes the last character entered, while the Clear button clears the entire line of digits, as displayed in the TextBox control. The ListBox control contains a list of previous conversions.

In the second tab page (Set Rates), the user can set the exchange rate for each currency using the ComboBox and TextBox controls.

Populating the Menu

Besides adding the various controls, you must add a Menu-Item control to the MainMenu control, as shown in Figure 3-4. When the user selects the Clear History menu item, it clears the ListBox control in the first tab page.

Coding the Controls

Now that the controls are set up, you need to begin writing the application logic that performs the currency translation.

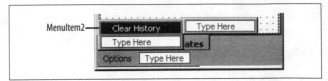

Figure 3-4. Adding the MenuItem control to the MainMenu

This application deals with three currencies and uses a single dataset object to bind the exchange rate of each currency to the ComboBox controls, where the end user selects the currencies to convert. To do this, switch to code view and declare the following DataSet object and a global Boolean variable:

```
Dim ds As New DataSet
Dim ready As Boolean = False
```

Now you need to tell the application where to get the exchange rate information. *Rates.xml* contains the exchange rate for each currency:

```
Const FILENAME="\My Documents\Personal\Rates.xml"
```

When the form is first loaded, you need to load the exchange rates by calling the LoadRates( ) method. After that, bind the dataset object using three different DataView objects to the three ComboBox controls:

```
Private Sub Form1_Load(ByVal sender As Object, _
                ByVal e As System.EventArgs) _
                Handles MyBase.Load
    LoadRates(ds)

    Dim viewFrom As New _
        DataView(ds.Tables("Currency"))
    Dim viewTo As New _
        DataView(ds.Tables("Currency"))
    Dim viewRate As New _
        DataView(ds.Tables("Currency"))

    ComboBox1.Items.Clear( )
    ComboBox1.DataSource = viewFrom
    ComboBox1.DisplayMember = "Sym"
    ComboBox1.ValueMember = "Rate"
```

```
          ComboBox2.Items.Clear()
          ComboBox2.DataSource = viewTo
          ComboBox2.DisplayMember = "Sym"
          ComboBox2.ValueMember = "Rate"

          ComboBox3.Items.Clear()
          ComboBox3.DataSource = ViewRate
          ComboBox3.DisplayMember = "Sym"
          ComboBox3.ValueMember = "Rate"

          ready = True
   End Sub
```

The LoadRates() method tries to load the exchange rate
information from the file *Rates.xml*, shown here:

```
<?xml version=1.0 standalone=yes?>
<NewDataSet>
   <Currency>
      <Sym>USD</Sym>
      <Rate>1</Rate>
   </Currency>
   <Currency>
      <Sym>CNY</Sym>
      <Rate>8</Rate>
   </Currency>
   <Currency>
      <Sym>SGD</Sym>
      <Rate>1.74</Rate>
   </Currency>
</NewDataSet>
```

The base currency is the U.S. dollar. All other currencies are
converted relative to the U.S. dollar. For example, $1 U.S. is
equivalent to about 1.69 Singapore dollars. Here is the code
for the LoadRates() subroutine:

```
Public Sub LoadRates(ByVal ds As DataSet)
    Try
        ds.ReadXml(FILENAME)
    Catch err As Exception
        InitRates(ds)
        ' init the rates if rates.xml
        ' cannot be found
    End Try
End Sub
```

The rates file does not exist when the application is first loaded, so the InitRates() method loads the exchange rates from a currency converter web service, such as the one located at *http://www.webservicex.com/CurrencyConvertor.asmx*. To use this web service—which converts the major currencies in the world—add a Web Reference to your project by right-clicking on your project name in Solution Explorer and then selecting Add Web Reference. The default proxy class name for this web service created by Visual Studio .NET is called com.webservicex.www.

The InitRates() method creates a dataset containing the currency table and three exchange rates obtained from the currency converter web service. If the web service is not reachable, a default exchange rate is used. The information is then written to file:

```
Public Sub InitRates(ByVal ds As DataSet)
    Dim ws As New _
      com.webservicex.www.CurrencyConvertor

    ds.Tables.Add("Currency")
    ds.Tables("Currency").Columns.Add("Sym")
    ds.Tables("Currency").Columns.Add("Rate")

    Dim row As DataRow
    row = ds.Tables("Currency").NewRow
    row("Sym") = "USD"
    row("Rate") = 1
    ds.Tables("Currency").Rows.Add(row)

    row = ds.Tables("Currency").NewRow
    row("Sym") = "CNY"
    Try
        row("Rate") = ws.ConversionRate( _
            com.webservicex.www.Currency.USD, _
            com.webservicex.www.Currency.CNY)
    Catch ex As Exception
        MsgBox("Error contacting web " & _
                "service. Setting to default " & _
                "rate.")
        row("Rate") = 8
```

```
      Finally
          ds.Tables("Currency").Rows.Add(row)
      End Try

      row = ds.Tables("Currency").NewRow
      row("Sym") = "SGD"
      Try
          row("Rate") = ws.ConversionRate( _
              com.webservicex.www.Currency.USD, _
              com.webservicex.www.Currency.SGD)
      Catch ex As Exception
          MsgBox("Error contacting web service." & _
                  " Setting to default rate.")
          row("Rate") = 1.74
      Finally
          ds.Tables("Currency").Rows.Add(row)
      End Try
      ds.WriteXml(FILENAME)
End Sub
```

Accepting Data Entry

Users enter the amount of currency they wish to convert
using the buttons 0 to 9 on the first tab page, which invokes
the cmdButtons() event. Note that this event is fired when-
ever one of the 11 buttons (0 to 9 and the decimal point button) is pushed. It must also perform error checking so that
users may not enter illegal entries, such as multiple decimal
points [.]. Once the button is clicked, the value appends the
TextBox control (txtValue) to show the user which numbers
she has entered:

```
Private Sub cmdButtons _
    (ByVal sender As System.Object, _
     ByVal e As System.EventArgs) _
     Handles cmd0.Click, cmd1.Click, cmd2.Click, _
     cmd3.Click, cmd4.Click, cmd5.Click, _
     cmd6.Click, cmd7.Click, cmd8.Click, _
     cmd9.Click, cmdPt.Click

     If txtValue.Text.Length > 7 Or _
       (txtValue.Text.IndexOf("0") = 0 And _
       CType(sender, Button).Text = "0") Or _
       (txtValue.Text.IndexOf(".") >= 0 And _
```

```
        CType(sender, Button).Text = ".") Then
        ' remove multiple "."
    Else
        If txtValue.Text.IndexOf("0") = 0 Then
            txtValue.Text = ""
        End If
        txtValue.Text += CType( _
            sender, Button).Text
    End If
End If
End Sub
```

When the value in the TextBox control is changed, indicating that the user has entered another number, the conversion amount must be recalculated. The UpdateValue( ) event handles recalculation when any of these events occur:

- The selection in ComboBox1 is changed (the currency to convert from).
- The selection in ComboBox2 is changed (the currency to convert to).
- The value in the TextBox control is changed.

Here is the UpdateValue( ) event:

```
Private Sub UpdateValue _
        (ByVal sender As System.Object, _
         ByVal e As System.EventArgs) _
         Handles ComboBox1.SelectedIndexChanged, _
         txtValue.TextChanged, _
         ComboBox2.SelectedIndexChanged
    If ready And txtValue.Text <> "" Then
        Try
            lblResult.Text = CSng(txtValue.Text) * _
                CSng(ComboBox2.SelectedValue) / _
                CSng(ComboBox1.SelectedValue)
        Catch ex As Exception
            'do nothing
        End Try
    End If
End Sub
```

The cmdBackSpace_Click( ) method is invoked when the Back Space button is clicked. It is used to remove the last digit that was entered:

```
Private Sub cmdBackSpace_Click _
            (ByVal sender As System.Object, _
            ByVal e As System.EventArgs) _
            Handles cmdBackSpace.Click

    ' length must be greater than 1 for deleting
    If txtValue.Text.Length > 0 Then
        txtValue.Text = Mid(txtValue.Text, 1, _
                        txtValue.Text.Length - 1)
    End If
    ' set to 0 if length is zero
    If txtValue.Text.Length = 0 Then
        txtValue.Text = 0
    End If
End Sub
```

The Clear button resets the TextBox control to the value 0:

```
Private Sub cmdClear_Click _
            (ByVal sender As System.Object, _
            ByVal e As System.EventArgs) _
            Handles cmdClear.Click
    txtValue.Text = 0
End Sub
```

The "=" button adds the current conversion into the ListBox control:

```
Private Sub cmdEq_Click _
            (ByVal sender As System.Object, _
            ByVal e As System.EventArgs) _
            Handles cmdEq.Click
    Dim str As String
    str = txtValue.Text & ComboBox1.Text & " = " _
        & lblResult.Text & ComboBox2.Text
    ListBox1.Items.Add(str)
End Sub
```

The Clear History menu item simply clears the items in the ListBox control:

```
Private Sub MenuItem2_Click _
            (ByVal sender As System.Object, _
            ByVal e As System.EventArgs) _
            Handles MenuItem2.Click
    ListBox1.Items.Clear()
End Sub
```

The second tab page control for the sample application allows the user to change the exchange rate of each currency. In production, this would frequently be done via the web service, which would grab the latest rates. In this case, users can override the rates included in the *Rates.xml* file. When ComboBox3 control is selected, the rate for the respective currency is displayed:

```
Private Sub ComboBox3_SelectedIndexChanged _
            (ByVal sender As System.Object, _
             ByVal e As System.EventArgs) _
            Handles ComboBox3.SelectedIndexChanged
    txtRate.Text = ds.Tables("Currency").Rows _
                (ComboBox3.SelectedIndex).Item _
                ("Rate").ToString
End Sub
```

The Update button will cause all the dataset objects to be updated and reflect the newly entered rate. It will then call the saveRate( ) method to save the changes to the *Rates.xml* file:

```
Private Sub cmdUpdate_Click _
            (ByVal sender As System.Object, _
             ByVal e As System.EventArgs) _
            Handles cmdUpdate.Click
    ds.Tables("Currency").Rows _
                (ComboBox3.SelectedIndex).Item _
                ("Rate") = txtRate.Text

    saveRate(ds)
End Sub
```

Finally, the saveRate( ) method saves the new exchange rates into the file:

```
Public Sub saveRate(ByVal ds As DataSet)
    ds.WriteXml(FILENAME)
    MsgBox("Rates saved.")
End Sub
```

That's it! Press F5 in Visual Studio to run the application. Figure 3-5 shows the Currency Converter in action.

A currency converter is just an example of the types of things you can do with .NET Compact Framework. If a currency converter is not what you need, you can extrapolate the logic

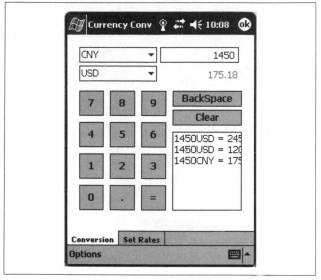

Figure 3-5. Using the Currency Converter

and tactics shown in this project in thousands of other ways.
For example, you've learned:

- How to use various built-in controls in .NET Compact
  Framework
- How to use datasets to manipulate XML documents
- How to use web services to retrieve information
- How to use XML documents as data storage
- How to program your controls to handle events

Project B: Book Ordering System

The next application illustrates several aspects of .NET Compact Framework Pocket PC programming—for example, consuming web services in the .NET Compact Framework, using the various controls in the .NET Compact Framework, and building a SQL Server CE database.

The application in this example allows a book salesperson to use a Pocket PC to search for books (using his company's web service) and then place orders for the books required by bookstores. The orders are then captured in a local SQL Server CE database for later perusal when the salesperson again connects to the corporate network.

Network Access from Your Pocket PC or Smartphone

There are a few ways for you to get network connectivity on your Pocket PC or Smartphone. For Pocket PCs, you may use:

Wi-Fi

> Simply get a Wi-Fi card and insert it into the CF or PCM-CIA slot on your Pocket PC. Many newer Pocket PCs come with built-in wireless capability.

Cellular

> Configure your Pocket PC to use GPRS or CDMA (using the infrared port or Bluetooth) through your cell phone.

Smartphone users should be able to use GPRS or CDMA directly, depending on their carrier's network.

Web Services

This web service uses the Pubs database in SQL Server or Microsoft SQL Server Desktop Engine (MSDE). The Pubs database comes preinstalled with SQL Server or MSDE, so it is easy for you to try out the code on your own machine.

If you don't have SQL Server installed, you can install MSDE, a lighter version of SQL Server, by selecting Start → All Programs → Microsoft .NET Framework SDK v1.1 and clicking Samples and QuickStart Tutorials (this will be available only if you installed the Framework SDK from the standalone installer or selected it during Visual Studio .NET setup). To install both MSDE and QuickStarts, follow the instructions on the web page that appears.

The web service simply contains one web method named getTitles(). The actual service name (in this case, Service1) may vary.

```vb
<%@ WebService Language="VB" Class="Service1" %>

Imports System
Imports System.Data
Imports System.Data.SqlClient
Imports System.Web.Services

Public Class Service1 : Inherits WebService

  <WebMethod()> _
  Public Function getTitles( _
    ByVal title As String) As DataSet

    ' Make the database connection.
    ' Replace USER and PASS with a
    ' valid username and password.
    Dim conn As New SqlConnection( _
      "server=localhost; uid=USER;" & _
      "password=PASS; database=Pubs")

    ' Create the SQL and set the parameter.
    Dim sql As String = "SELECT * FROM " & _
      "titles WHERE title LIKE @title"
    Dim comm As New SqlCommand(sql, conn)
    comm.Parameters.Add("@title", _
                        "%" & title & "%")

    ' Create a data adapter and data set.
    Dim dataAdapter As New SqlDataAdapter(comm)
    Dim ds As New DataSet()

    ' Fill the data set with the query results.
    conn.Open()
    dataAdapter.Fill(ds, "titles")
    conn.Close()

    ' Return the dataset.
    Return ds

  End Function

End Class
```

The getTitles( ) web method takes in a search string input parameter and returns a dataset containing the titles that match the search string.

If you are using MSDE, you will need to specify the name of the instance in the Connection string and use integrated security, as in:

```
Dim conn As New SqlConnection( _
    "server=(local)\NetSDK;" & _
    "Integrated Security=SSPI;" & _
    "database=pubs;" )
```

Use Visual Studio .NET 2003 to create this web service (New Project → Visual Basic Projects → ASP.NET Web Service), and host it at a location where the Pocket PC or Pocket PC Emulator can reach it. You should be able to host it on the same machine on which you are running Visual Studio .NET and the emulator.

Press F5 to build and test the web service. Make sure it works correctly before moving on to the next step. You should also make a note of the web service's URL, such as *http://localhost/WebService1/Service1.asmx*.

Creating the Pocket PC Application

With the web service created, you should now create the Pocket PC application.

The Pocket PC application consists of a tab control with two tab pages (see "Project A: Currency Converter" for instructions on creating tab pages). The first tab page allows the salesperson to check for book titles and place orders at bookstores. The second tab page lists the orders, sorted by bookstore.

You must add the controls listed in Table 3-2 to this form (see Figures 3-6 and 3-7 for the layout).

Table 3-2. Controls used in the bookstore application

Control type	Check Titles tab	View Orders tab
Label	lblStoreName, lblTitleID, lblPrice, "Store ID", "Name", "Search", "Result", "Title ID", "Price", "Qty"	"Store IDs", "Orders"
TextBox	txtSearch, txtQty	
ComboBox	cboStoreID, cboResult	
Button	cmdSearch, cmdAdd	cmdRefresh
ListBox		lstStoreIDs, lstOrders
MultiLine TextBox	txtNotes	

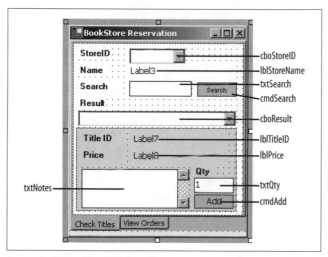

Figure 3-6. The Check Titles tab page

TIP

To ensure that the SIP (the virtual keyboard) is displayed when the user wants to enter text into a TextBox control, there must be at least one MainMenu control in your form (there should already be one there by default).

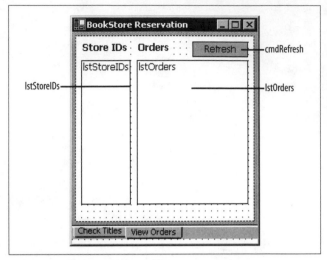

Figure 3-7. The View Orders tab page

When the form is first loaded, it must check if the Pocket PC contains the database for storing bookstore information. If it doesn't, it uses the SQL Server CE Engine object to create the database. To connect to a SQL Server CE database, you need to use the SQL Server CE Managed Provider. So the first thing you need to do is add a Reference to the *System.Data. SqlServerCe.dll* assembly (right-click on the solution in the Solution Explorer and select Add Reference). You then need to import the relevant namespaces:

```
Imports System.Data.SqlServerCe
Imports System.IO
```

Once you have created the database, you need to create tables using the ADO.NET classes in the SQL Server CE Managed Provider (the SqlCeConnection and SqlCeCommand). The following code checks for the database, creates it if it doesn't exist, and creates the table:

```
'-----conn and ds are defined globally-----
Dim conn As New SqlCeConnection( _
 "Data Source=\My Documents\BookStores.sdf")
Dim ds As DataSet
'-------------------------------------------
Sub createStoreDB()
    ' if database does not exist, create one
    If Not File.Exists( _
      "\My Documents\BookStores.sdf") Then
        Dim sqlCeEngine As New SqlCeEngine( _
          "Data Source=" & _
          "\My Documents\BookStores.sdf")
        sqlCeEngine.CreateDatabase()

        Dim cmd As New SqlCeCommand( _
          "CREATE TABLE Stores(storeID int " & _
          "Primary Key NOT NULL, " & _
          "storeName nvarchar(20))", conn)
        conn.Open()
        cmd.ExecuteNonQuery()
        cmd.CommandText = _
          "CREATE TABLE Orders(storeID int, " & _
          "title_id nvarchar(20), qty int)"
        cmd.ExecuteNonQuery()

        cmd.CommandText = _
          "INSERT INTO Stores (storeID, " & _
          "storeName) VALUES (1, " & _
          "'Great BookStore')"
        cmd.ExecuteNonQuery()

        cmd.CommandText = _
          "INSERT INTO Stores (storeID, " & _
          "storeName) VALUES (2, " & _
          "'Computer BookStore')"
        cmd.ExecuteNonQuery()
        conn.Close()
    End If

End Sub
Private Sub Form1_Load _
    (ByVal sender As System.Object, _
     ByVal e As System.EventArgs) _
     Handles MyBase.Load
   createStoreDB() ' create DB if not present
   LoadStores() ' load all the stores available
End Sub
```

This code created and populated two tables: Stores and Orders. The Stores table contains the list of bookstores, and the Orders table captures the orders made by bookstores. Figure 3-8 shows the relationship between these tables.

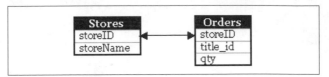

Figure 3-8. Relationship between the Stores and Orders tables

The next step is to load the bookstore list into the Combo-Box control using the SqlCeDataReader class:

```
Sub LoadStores()
  conn.Open()
  Dim reader As SqlCeDataReader
  Dim cmd As New SqlCeCommand( _
    "SELECT * FROM Stores", conn)
  reader = cmd.ExecuteReader
  While reader.Read
      cboStoreID.Items.Add( _
        reader.Item("storeID"))
  End While
  conn.Close()
End Sub
```

So, when the form is loaded, the ComboBox is filled with the bookstore list, as shown in Figure 3-9.

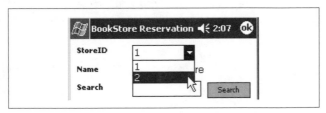

Figure 3-9. Populating the ComboBox

When a Store ID is selected, it will display the name of that store:

```
Private Sub cboStoreID_SelectedIndexChanged( _
  ByVal sender As System.Object, _
  ByVal e As System.EventArgs) _
  Handles cboStoreID.SelectedIndexChanged
    conn.Open()
    Dim sql As String = _
      "SELECT * FROM Stores WHERE storeID=" & _
      cboStoreID.Items(cboStoreID.SelectedIndex)
    Dim cmd As New SqlCeCommand(sql, conn)
    Dim reader As _
      SqlCeDataReader = cmd.ExecuteReader
    reader.Read()
    lblStoreName.Text = reader.Item("storeName")
    conn.Close()
End Sub
```

Consuming the Web Service

When you tested the web service earlier in this section, you
should have made a note of the address, which was probably
something like *http://localhost/WebService1/Service1.asmx*.
You must replace the *localhost* in the web service's name
with the machine's hostname or IP address, because *localhost* always resolves to the local machine (or device, including one running under an emulator).

To search for specific titles, this application will use the web
service we created earlier. Select the project in the Solution
Explorer, right-click on it, choose Add Web Reference, and
supply the path to the service's WSDL.

The result of the web service is bound to the Result Combo-
Box. You may need to replace WebReference.Service1 with a
different name, depending on how you named the service:

```
Private Sub cmdSearch_Click( _
  ByVal sender As System.Object, _
  ByVal e As System.EventArgs) _
  Handles cmdSearch.Click
    Dim ws As New WebReference.Service1()
    ' get the web service
    ds = ws.getTitles(txtSearch.Text)
    cboResult.DataSource = ds.Tables(0)
    cboResult.DisplayMember = "title"
End Sub
```

When a title is selected, detailed information about the selected title is displayed, as shown in Figure 3-10.

Figure 3-10. Displaying information about the selected title

```
Private Sub cboResult_SelectedIndexChanged( _
    ByVal sender As System.Object, _
    ByVal e As System.EventArgs) _
    Handles cboResult.SelectedIndexChanged
    ' display the information of the
    ' selected book.
    Dim row As DataRow
    row = ds.Tables("titles").Rows( _
      cboResult.SelectedIndex)
    lblTitleID.Text = row.Item("title_id")
    lblPrice.Text = "$" & row.Item("price")
    txtNotes.Text = row.Item("notes")
End Sub
```

To place an order for a bookstore, specify the quantity and click the Add button. An order for the selected bookstore will be added.

```
Private Sub cmdAdd_Click( _
  ByVal sender As System.Object, _
  ByVal e As System.EventArgs) _
  Handles cmdAdd.Click
    If Not IsNumeric(txtQty.Text) Then
      MsgBox("Quantity must be a number.")
    Else
      '---add the title to the stores ORDER table
      conn.Open()
```

```
        Dim sql As String = _
          "INSERT INTO Orders " & _
          "(storeID, title_id, Qty) VALUES (" & _
          cboStoreID.Items( _
          cboStoreID.SelectedIndex) _
          & ",'" & _
          lblTitleID.Text & "'," & _
          txtQty.Text & ")"
        Dim cmd As New SqlCeCommand(sql, conn)
        cmd.ExecuteNonQuery()
        MsgBox("Title added for " & _
              lblStoreName.Text, _
              MsgBoxStyle.Information, _
              "Orders")
        conn.Close()
      End If
  End Sub
```

A message box confirms the addition, as shown in Figure 3-11.

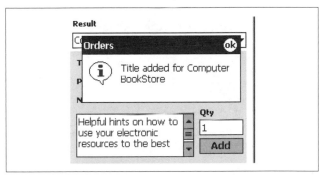

Figure 3-11. Confirming the addition

Checking the Orders

Clicking on the second tab page displays the orders made by bookstores. When the Refresh button is clicked, the first ListBox control will display the list of available bookstores:

```
    Private Sub cmdRefresh_Click( _
      ByVal sender As System.Object, _
      ByVal e As System.EventArgs) _
      Handles cmdRefresh.Click
```

```
    '---displays the list of stores available
    conn.Open()
    Dim sql As String = "SELECT * FROM Stores"
    Dim cmd As New SqlCeCommand(sql, conn)
    Dim reader As SqlCeDataReader = _
      cmd.ExecuteReader
    '---clears the listbox
    lstStoreIDs.Items.Clear()
    While reader.Read()
        lstStoreIDs.Items.Add( _
          reader.Item("storeID"))
    End While
    conn.Close()
End Sub
```

When a particular bookstore is selected, its corresponding order is then listed on the second ListBox control, as shown in Figure 3-12:

```
Private Sub lstStoreIDs_SelectedIndexChanged( _
  ByVal sender As System.Object, _
  ByVal e As System.EventArgs) _
  Handles lstStoreIDs.SelectedIndexChanged
    '---displays the orders of store selected
    conn.Open()
    Dim sql As String = _
     "SELECT * FROM Orders WHERE storeID=" & _
     lstStoreIDs.Items(lstStoreIDs.SelectedIndex)
    Dim cmd As New SqlCeCommand(sql, conn)
    Dim reader As SqlCeDataReader = _
      cmd.ExecuteReader()
    '---clears the listbox
    lstOrders.Items.Clear()
    While reader.Read()
        lstOrders.Items.Add( _
          reader.Item("title_id") & " - " & _
          reader.Item("qty") & "-copy(ies)")
    End While
    conn.Close()
End Sub
```

Using the SQL Server CE Query Analyzer

SQL Server CE 2.0 comes with a tool known as the SQL Server CE Query Analyzer. The first time you run an application with the SQL Server CE Managed Provider referenced, Visual Studio

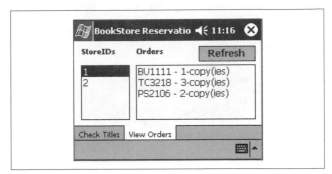

Figure 3-12. Viewing the orders

.NET will copy the relevant files to the target device (or emulator). The SQL Server CE Query Analyzer can then be invoked by clicking Start → SQLCE Query (as shown in Figure 3-13).

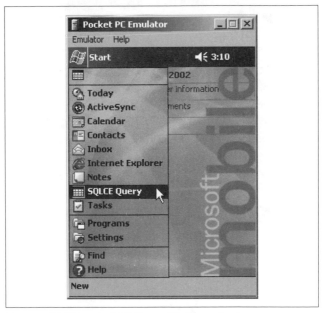

Figure 3-13. Using the SQL Server CE Query Analyzer

To connect to a SQL Server CE database, click the button shown with a green arrow and a cylinder, as shown in Figure 3-14.

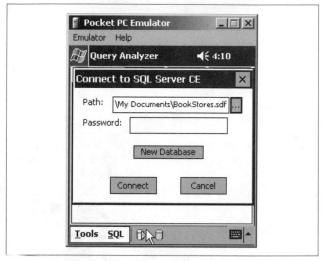

Figure 3-14. Connecting to a SQL Server CE database

You can either connect to an existing database or create a new one. Figure 3-15 shows the tables and fields of the database from the Bookstore application.

To retrieve the records in the tables, you can use SQL statements under the SQL tab and examine the results under the Grid tab, as shown in Figure 3-16.

A nice feature of the Query Analyzer is the Button Presets function, which allows you to store commonly used SQL statements so that they can be invoked by simply clicking on the preset buttons (labeled 1–10), as shown in Figure 3-17.

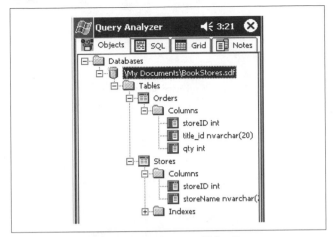

Figure 3-15. Examining the BookStores.sdf database

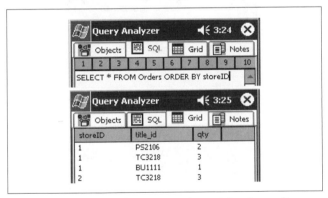

Figure 3-16. Using SQL Statements and examining the results

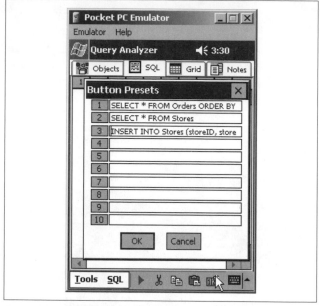

Figure 3-17. Using the Button Presets

Project C: Bluetooth Chat

Bluetooth is one of today's most exciting technologies. It is a short-range radio wave wireless technology operating in the 2.4 GHz frequency spectrum. With an operating range of 30 feet (10 meters) and a maximum transmission rate of 1 Mbps, Bluetooth is widely touted as a "cable replacement" solution.

Bluetooth has been around for awhile, but there seem to be few developers who have experience in building applications that will run over Bluetooth. This project shows how you can build a Bluetooth chat application using the .NET Compact Framework. Once you've built a chat application using this simple example, you should have a good foundation for building any number of killer Bluetooth applications.

The chat application project lets two users with Bluetooth-enabled Pocket PCs communicate with each other—as long as they are within the 30-foot range of Bluetooth. It is useful as a communication tool during meetings, where private conversations can take place without affecting the meeting, or as a mobile substitute for an instant messenger.

Two Pocket PC devices from HP were used to build and test the chat application: an iPAQ 3870 (with Bluetooth built-in) and an iPAQ 3630 (with the Bluetooth Expansion Pack for the iPAQ 3630). These Pocket PCs are shown in Figure 3-18.

Figure 3-18. The two Pocket PCs used for testing this example

Here's what you need to try this one out:

- Visual Studio .NET 2003.
- Two Pocket PCs with Bluetooth capabilities. (Most new Pocket PCs today ship with Bluetooth capability. For Pocket PCs without built-in Bluetooth, you can usually purchase Bluetooth expansion jackets or cards.)
- Microsoft ActiveSync 3.6 or higher.

Building the User Interface

To create the sample application, start Visual Studio .NET 2003 and create a new Smart Device Application project.

First, populate the default Form1 with the following controls:

- Two TextBoxes (txtMessage and txtMessageLog)
- One Button (cmdSend)
- One MainMenu (labeled Settings)
- Two MenuItems (labeled Connect and Disconnect)

For txtMessageLog, use the Properties dialog to set Multiline to True and ScrollBars to Vertical. The populated Form1 is shown in Figure 3-19.

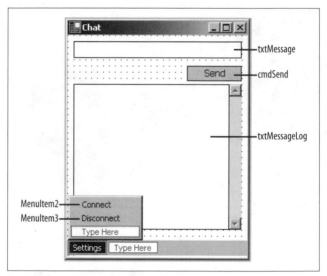

Figure 3-19. Form1 from the Chat application

Communicating Using Bluetooth

Windows CE 3.0—the operating system for Pocket PC 2000 and 2002 devices—does not come with any APIs for Bluetooth communication. Consequently, you have to use other methods, such as platform invoke, to communicate using Bluetooth. The lack of an API for Bluetooth means that you cannot program Bluetooth communications in the same way you use sockets for TCP/IP communications. Instead, Bluetooth is just another serial port. Therefore, Bluetooth communication is actually done via serial connections. You can see for yourself by going to Bluetooth Manager → Tools → Settings for All Devices → Serial Port in your Pocket PC's main menu (see Figure 3-20).

Managed Classes for Bluetooth Communications?

The .NET Compact Framework does not supply managed class libraries for Bluetooth communication. So if you are going to work with Bluetooth, you need to either improvise Bluetooth communications using serial communications (just like what you did in this project), or use the Bluetooth APIs provided in the operating system. Windows CE .NET—the operating system for Windows Mobile—does provide Bluetooth APIs for Bluetooth communication. Check out the Windows CE .NET documentation for more information on which APIs to use.

The Bluetooth connection is actually mapped to two COM ports—one for incoming traffic and one for outgoing traffic. On my test device, the incoming port is COM7 and the outgoing port is COM8 (see Figure 3-20). I will program the Bluetooth application using serial communication techniques.

TIP

You need to check the COM port number on your Pocket PC. Change the port number in the code to match that of your devices.

Unfortunately, the .NET Compact Framework class library does not contain managed classes for serial communication.

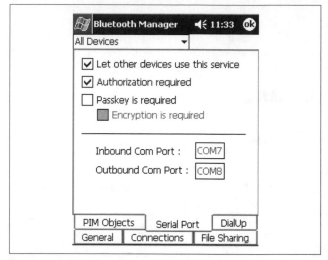

Figure 3-20. The Bluetooth connection is just another pair of serial ports

You have to rely on the operating system calls to provide that. In particular, you need to make use of functions provided by Windows CE 3.0's *coredll.dll* library.

In the .NET Compact Framework, use the <DllImport()> attribute to import the library that you want to use. For example, here are four imported functions from the *coredll.dll* library:

CreateFile()
  Opens a connection to a COM port

ReadFile()
  Reads data from a COM port

WriteFile()
  Writes data to a COM port

CloseHandle()
  Closes a COM port

Many of the details involved in serial communications, including complete error handling, are not included in this project. For more information on building serial-comm applications in Windows CE, refer to *http://msdn.microsoft. com/library/default.asp?url=/library/en-us/wceseril/html/ cmconProgrammingSerialConnections.asp* and *http://msdn. microsoft.com/library/en-us/dnnetcomp/html/PISAPICF.asp*.

The VB.NET code for the import is:

```
Imports System.Runtime.InteropServices
```

The following should be declared within the class definition of the Windows Form:

```
<DllImport("coredll.dll")> _
Private Shared Function CreateFile _
     (ByVal lpFileName As String, _
      ByVal dwDesiredAccess As Integer, _
      ByVal dwShareMode As Integer, _
      ByVal lpSecurityAttributes As Integer, _
      ByVal dwCreationDisposition As Integer, _
      ByVal dwFlagsAndAttributes As Integer, _
      ByVal hTemplateFile As Integer) As Integer
End Function

<DllImport("coredll.dll")> _
Private Shared Function ReadFile _
     (ByVal hFile As Integer, _
      ByVal Buffer() As Byte, _
      ByVal nNumberOfBytesToRead As Integer, _
      ByRef lpNumberOfBytesRead As Integer, _
      ByRef lpOverlapped As Integer) As Integer
End Function

<DllImport("coredll.dll")> _
Private Shared Function WriteFile _
     (ByVal hFile As Integer, _
      ByVal Buffer() As Byte, _
      ByVal nNumberOfBytesToWrite As Integer, _
      ByRef lpNumberOfBytesWritten As Integer, _
      ByVal lpOverlapped As Integer) As Boolean
End Function
```

```
<DllImport("coredll.dll")> _
Private Shared Function CloseHandle _
    (ByVal hObject As Integer) As Integer
End Function
```

Now that you have the needed functions, you can begin
building the application. Start by declaring some global
variables:

```
Dim infileHandler As Long
Dim outfileHandler As Long
Dim numReadWrite As Integer
Dim t1 As System.Threading.Thread
Dim stopThread As Boolean = False
```

You need to create a Connect menu item that, when tapped,
will call the connect( ) method to open the serial connections. You need to open the connections to the inbound and
outbound port so that data can be both received and sent.
The following code handles the Connect menu selection:

```
Private Sub MenuItem2_Click _
    (ByVal sender As System.Object, _
     ByVal e As System.EventArgs) _
    Handles MenuItem2.Click
    connect()
    '---disable the Connect item
    MenuItem2.Enabled = False
    '---enable the Disconnect item
    MenuItem3.Enabled = True
End Sub
```

The method we are using for reading incoming messages,
ReadFile( ), is a blocking one. Therefore, we need to invoke
a thread to continuously poll for incoming data while allow-
ing our application to be responsive to users' input at the
same time. This is done in the connect( ) method:

```
Public Sub connect()
    '---port number for Bluetooth connection
    Dim inPort As Short = 7
    Dim outPort As Short = 8

    '---Opens the port for Bluetooth
    infileHandler = CreateFile _
```

```
                        ("COM" & inPort & ":", _
                        &HC0000000, 0, 0, 3, 0, 0)
    Application.DoEvents()
    outfileHandler = CreateFile _
                    ("COM" & outPort & ":", _
                    &HC0000000, 0, 0, 3, 0, 0)
    Application.DoEvents()

    '---invoke the thread to receive
    '---incoming messages
    stopThread = False
    t1 = New Threading.Thread _
        (AddressOf receiveLoop)
    t1.Start()
End Sub
```

The send( ) method writes a message to the COM port using the WriteFile( ) method. After a message is sent, a copy of the message is added to the TextBox control:

```
Public Function send(ByVal message As String) _
        As Integer
    '---send the message through the serial port
    Dim value As String = message & vbCrLf
    Dim retCode As Integer = WriteFile _
                    (outfileHandler, _
                     stringToByteArray(value), _
                     value.Length(), _
                     numRcadWrite, _
                     0)
    txtMessageLog.Text += value
    Return retCode
End Function
```

The receiveLoop( ) method continuously polls for incoming messages. As Windows controls are not thread-safe, accessing Windows controls within a thread will have unpredictable results. Therefore, you need to use a delegate method to call the updateMessage( ) method to update the TextBox control with the received message:

```
Public Sub receiveLoop()
    '---receive the message through
    '---the serial port
```

```
    Dim inbuff(300) As Byte
    Dim retCode As Integer = ReadFile _
                    (infileHandler, _
                     inbuff, _
                     inbuff.Length, _
                     numReadWrite, _
                     0)
    Application.DoEvents()
    While True
        If retCode = 0 Or stopThread Then
        '---either error or stop is requested
            Exit While
        Else
            Dim updateDelegate As New _
                MyDelegate _
                (AddressOf updateMessageLog)

            updateDelegate.Invoke _
                (byteArrayToString(inbuff))
            ReDim inbuff(300)
            retCode = ReadFile(infileHandler, _
                              inbuff, _
                              inbuff.Length, _
                              numReadWrite, _
                              0)
            Application.DoEvents()
        End If
    End While
End Sub
```

The myDelegate() method has the same signature as the
updateMessageLog() method. myDelegate() is called when
updating the TextBox control. You should not directly call
the updateMessageLog() within the thread; only the main
thread can directly call it.

```
    Public Delegate Sub myDelegate(ByVal str _
                    As String)
    Public Sub updateMessageLog(ByVal str As String)
        If str.Length > 0 Then
            txtMessageLog.Text += "-->" & str
        End If
    End Sub
```

Clicking the Send button invokes the send( ) method:

```
Private Sub cmdSend_Click(ByVal sender _
                 As System.Object, _
                 ByVal e As System.EventArgs) _
                 Handles cmdSend.Click
    If send(txtMessageLog.Text) = 0 Then
        MsgBox("Error sending message.")
    End If
End Sub
```

Finally, clicking on the Disconnect menu item invokes the disconnect( ) method:

```
Private Sub MenuItem3_Click(ByVal sender As _
                 System.Object, _
                 ByVal e As System.EventArgs) _
                 Handles MenuItem3.Click
    disconnect()
    '---enable the Connect button
    MenuItem2.Enabled = True
    '---disable the Connect button
    MenuItem3.Enabled = False
End Sub
```

The disconnect( ) method will set a global flag for the thread to stop receiving incoming messages. It will also close the two open ports.

```
Public Sub disconnect()
    stopThread = True
    CloseHandle(infileHandler)
    CloseHandle(outfileHandler)
End Sub
```

Byte to String and Back Again

Throughout this application, we have used two supporting methods: stringToByteArray( ) and byteArrayToString( ). They are necessary because the ReadFile( ) and WriteFile( ) methods both take in a byte array containing the message to be read and sent, respectively.

The stringToByteArray( ) method converts a string into a byte array:

```
Public Function stringToByteArray _
    (ByVal str As String) As Byte()
    '---e.g. "abcdefg" to {a,b,c,d,e,f,g}
    Dim s As Char()
    s = str.ToCharArray
    Dim b(s.Length - 1) As Byte
    Dim i As Integer
    For i = 0 To s.Length - 1
        b(i) = Convert.ToByte(s(i))
    Next
    Return b
End Function
```

The byteArrayToString( ) method converts a byte array into a string:

```
Function byteArrayToString _
        (ByVal b( ) As Byte) As String
    '---e.g. {a,b,c,d,e,f,g} to "abcdefg"
    Dim str As String
    Dim enc As System.Text.ASCIIEncoding
    enc = New System.Text.ASCIIEncoding
    str = enc.GetString(b, 0, b.Length( ))
    Return str
End Function
```

When sending a message, it needs to be converted to a byte array, and vice versa; when a message is received as a byte array, it needs to be converted back to a string so it can be displayed on the device.

TIP

An alternative way to convert a string to byte array (and vice versa) would be to use the Encoding.ASCII. GetString( ) and Encoding.ASCII.GetBytes( ) methods available in the System.Text namespace.

Testing the Application

To test the application, you need to install the sample application on both Pocket PCs. The easiest way to do this is to connect one of the Pocket PCs to your development machine and use Visual Studio .NET 2003 to deploy the application on the device. Press F5 to automatically copy the application, and select the appropriate device when prompted.

The next step is to copy the application onto the other Pocket PC. There are two steps involved here. First, you need to generate a Cabinet (CAB) file for the application so it can be copied and installed on the target Pocket PC. Second, you need to install the .NET Compact Framework on it (this needs to be done only once, and only if the .NET Compact Framework didn't come preinstalled).

But before you can do either task, you need to establish a Bluetooth connection between the two Pocket PCs—the Bluetooth Manager creates a bond between them (see Figure 3-21).

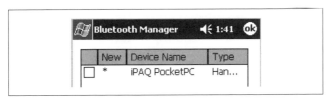

Figure 3-21. Making a Bluetooth connection

Now that the two devices recognize each other, you can send the CAB file and the framework to the remote device. To generate a CAB file for your application, click on the Build Cab File button in Visual Studio .NET 2003 (see Figure 3-22).

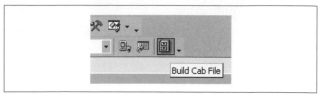

Figure 3-22. Generate a CAB file for your application

When the CAB file is generated, you can find it in the *Cab\ Debug* folder of your application. Visual Studio .NET 2003 generates CAB files for the various platforms that are supported by the .NET Compact Framework (see Figure 3-23). Make sure to identify the right one for your platform.

Figure 3-23. Pick a CAB

To copy the CAB file to your Pocket PC, connect the Pocket PC to your machine and use Microsoft ActiveSync's Explore option. Drag and drop the CAB file onto the desired directory (see Figure 3-24).

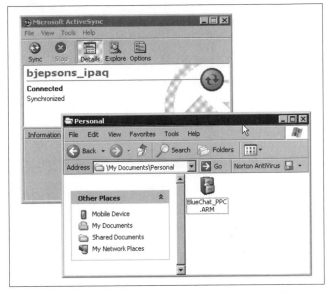

Figure 3-24. Copy the CAB file to your device using ActiveSync

Once the CAB file is copied to the device, you can use Bluetooth to send the CAB file to the other Pocket PC, as shown in Figure 3-25.

The next step is to copy the .NET Compact Framework to the Pocket PC. You can find the CAB file for the .NET Compact Framework in the following directory on your development machine (with Visual Studio .NET 2003 installed):

```
\Program Files\Microsoft Visual Studio .NET 2003\
CompactFrameworkSDK\v1.0.5000\Windows CE\wce300
```

Choose the appropriate platform for your Pocket PC (see Figure 3-26).

For example, the second Pocket PC is an iPAQ 3630, so choose the "arm" platform since it runs on an ARM processor. (To determine the type of processor on which your

Figure 3-25. Use the Bluetooth Manager to transfer the CAB file from one device to the other

Figure 3-26. Choose your processor

Pocket PC is running, go to Start → Settings, tap on the System tab, and click the About icon. Under the Processor category, you should see the processor type. Both of my Pocket PCs run on the ARM SA1110 processor.)

Copy the *netcf.core.ppc3.arm* file (or the appropriate one for your device) to the Pocket PC via ActiveSync. Again, use Bluetooth to send the file from one device to the other.

On the other Pocket PC, you can now install the .NET Compact Framework and the application by tapping on the two CAB files (see Figure 3-27). The order of installation is important—install the .NET Compact Framework first (this will be necessary only if your second device is a Windows CE 3.0-based device; Windows Mobile devices will have the .NET Compact Framework included).

Figure 3-27. Installing the .NET Compact Framework and the sample application

Once the application is installed, you should find a BluetoothChat application icon in the Programs folder (see Figure 3-28).

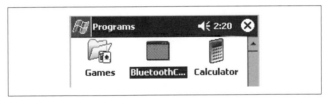

Figure 3-28. Locating the Chat application icon

Before you load the application, make sure that you have a Bluetooth bonding between the two Pocket PCs. Tap on the Settings → Connect menu item to establish a serial connection. The other Pocket PC will receive an authorization request for the use of the serial port. Click Accept. Launch your BluetoothChat application and select the Connect menu item to start chatting (see Figure 3-29).

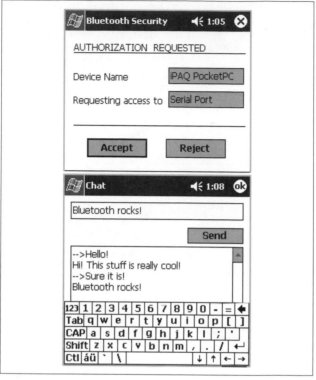

Figure 3-29. Two Pocket PCs engaged in a chat

PART IV

Deploying .NET Compact Framework Applications

Now that you have seen the various Pocket PC projects detailed in Part III, it's time to deploy them onto your devices. There are several ways in which you can deploy your applications:

Web site
> Users can connect to a web site that hosts the installation files for your application.

File share
> Users can connect to a shared folder on a computer and install the application directly from the server.

Send to another device
> You can send the installation files of your application from one device to another through an infrared or Bluetooth connection.

Memory storage cards
> Your application can be stored on memory storage cards. Users can install your application by inserting the memory cards into their devices.

ActiveSync
> You can use ActiveSync to perform the installation. There are two ways to do this through ActiveSync—by directly copying the installation files onto the device or by using the WinCE Application Manager.

This part shows how to prepare your application for deployment and how to deploy it onto real devices.

Packaging CAB Files

Regardless of which method you choose to deploy your application, you first need to package your application into CAB files. The CAB files are then deployed to devices and are expanded and installed.

Modifying Your Project Information

Before you build the CAB files for your application, you need to change the configuration of your application from Debug mode to Release mode (see Figure 4-1).

Figure 4-1. Changing the configuration from Debug to Release mode

You can also change the icon used for your application by right-clicking on the project name in Solution Explorer and then selecting Properties. Click the Build item (on the left of the window) and select a new icon (see Figure 4-2).

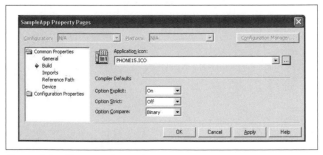

Figure 4-2. Changing the application icon

You can also change the output folder for your application. The output folder specifies the folder where your application will be installed on the device (see Figure 4-3).

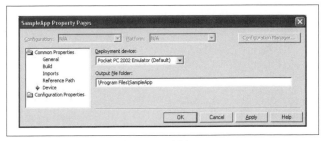

Figure 4-3. Configuring the output folder

Building CAB Files

To build the CAB files for your project, click on Build → Build Cab File (see Figure 4-4).

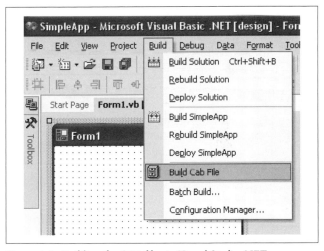

Figure 4-4. Building the CAB files in Visual Studio .NET

In the *Cab\Debug* folder of your project, you will see a list of CAB files generated for the various processor platforms (see Figure 4-5).

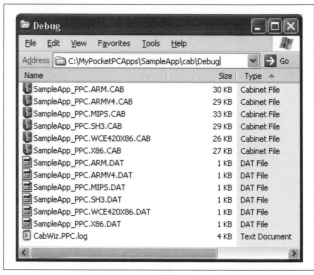

Figure 4-5. List of CAB files for the various processor platforms

What About Platform Independence?

Since .NET Compact Framework applications compile to the platform-independent MSIL (Microsoft Intermediate Language), why is it necessary to build separate CAB files for each processor platform? The reason is that your application might use platform-specific functions. Hence, Visual Studio .NET generates the CAB files for all platforms that support your application. As an example, if your application uses APIs that are supported only on certain platforms, then only the CAB files for those supported platforms will be generated.

In the *Obj\Release* folder, you will also find the *SampleApp_PPC.inf* and *BuildCab.bat* files (see Figure 4-6). You can customize your application's installation settings using this *.inf* file. The *BuildCab.bat* batch file allows you to rebuild your CAB files after you have made changes to the *.inf* file.

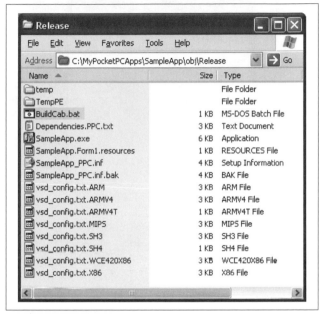

Figure 4-6. Locating the batch file and the .inf file

Let's modify the *.inf* file. The changes to the original are displayed in bold:

```
[Version]
Signature="$Windows NT$"
Provider="Active Developer"
CESignature="$Windows CE$"
...
...
[Shortcuts]
AD's SampleApp,0,SampleApp.exe,%CE17%
```

The macro string %ce17% installs the application into the \Windows\Start Menu directory in your Pocket PC. This will essentially make your application item visible in the Start menu (see Figure 4-7).

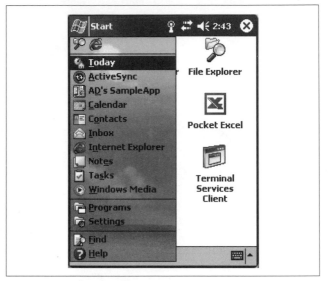

Figure 4-7. Locating the application in the Start menu

If you want to install into the \Windows\Start Menu\Programs directory instead, you should use the %ce11% macro string.

TIP

See the article "Creating an .inf File" for more information on the various macro strings: *http://msdn.microsoft. com/library/default.asp?url=/library/en-us/wcepb40/html/ cxconCreatingInfFile.asp*

Once the changes have been made, you need to rebuild your CAB files by running *BuildCab.bat*:

```
C:\MyPocketPCApps\SampleApp\obj\Release>BuildCab

C:\MyPocketPCApps\SampleApp\obj\Release>"C:\Program Files\
Microsoft Visual Studio .NET 2003\CompactFrameworkSDK\v1.
0.5000\Windows CE\..\bin\..\bin\cabwiz.exe" "C:\
MyPocketPCApps\SampleApp\obj\Release\SampleApp_PPC.inf"
/dest "C:\MyPocketPCApps\SampleApp\cab\Release" /err
CabWiz.PPC.log /cpu ARMV4 ARM SH3 MIPS X86 WCE420X86
```

Determining the Right Processor Type for Your Device

Given the many Pocket PC devices in the market today, you may not know the exact type of processor used in your Pocket PC. Here is a guide to help you identify the right processor:

- Pocket PC or Pocket PC 2000 devices probably use ARM processors. However, there are other Pocket PCs with SH3 and MIPS processors, too. Check with your manufacturer for more details. The OS is Windows CE 3.0.
- Pocket PC 2002 devices use ARM processors exclusively. The OS is Windows CE 3.0.
- Pocket PC 2003 devices use ARM4 processors exclusively. The OS is Windows CE .NET 4.1 or 4.2.

Installing the CAB Files

To deploy the CAB files, you can use ActiveSync to copy them onto the Pocket PC. Use ActiveSync's Explore feature (see Figure 4-8) to display the directory of your Pocket PC. Simply copy the CAB file (and any other supporting files, such as databases and XML files) over, use File Explorer on your Pocket PC to navigate to the folder containing the CAB file, and tap on it to install the application.

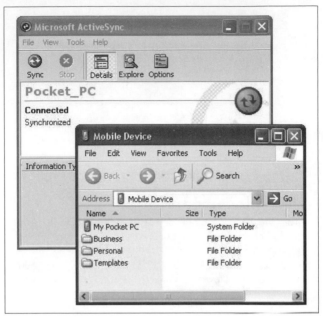

Figure 4-8. Using the ActiveSync's Explore feature to copy files

---

TIP

Your application requires the .NET Compact Framework to be installed on the target device. See the next section on how to obtain and install the .NET Compact Framework on the device (if it is not already installed).

Redistributing the .NET Compact Framework

As mentioned in Part I, not all devices have the .NET Compact Framework. However, most new devices come with the .NET Compact Framework preinstalled in ROM.

For devices that do not come with the .NET Compact Framework preinstalled, you need to distribute the free .NET Compact Framework together with your application. You can download the .NET Compact Framework Redistributable from *http://www.microsoft.com/downloads/*.

TIP

The .NET Compact Framework Redistributable uses ActiveSync to install the .NET Compact Framework onto the device.

Deploying to the Emulator

You can deploy your CAB files to your emulator by copying the CAB files to a shared folder on your PC. On your emulator, use File Explorer to mount the shared folder (see Figure 4-9), and copy the CAB files onto the local filesystem. To install the application on your emulator, navigate to the folder containing the CAB files and tap on each one.

You can also use this technique to apply the latest service packs for the .NET Compact Framework.

Deploying Smartphone Applications

Deploying Smartphone applications is very different from deploying applications for Pocket PCs and PCs. In the case of Smartphone, you should not presume that the user has a PC through which to install new software. Thus, installing applications through ActiveSync is not always possible. Instead, you should rely on the common ways a phone user interacts with the world outside the phone. There are three possibilities—through the Web, through SMS, and through email. This section demonstrates how to distribute a Smartphone application through the Web.

Figure 4-9. Mounting a shared folder on your emulator

Create a new Smart Device application project and save it as
C:\MySmartphoneApps\SimpleApp. You will build this application and then distribute it to your users.

Creating Installers

Most Pocket PC users are familiar with using ActiveSync to install applications. You connect your Pocket PC to your PC via ActiveSync and run the setup application. The WinCE Application Manager is then launched to install and uninstall the application on the Pocket PC.

You can create installers for your Pocket PC application so that the user would just need to run a setup application, and everything will be taken care of automatically. However, creating installers require you to build custom components for the installation. For an example, check out the article "Developing and Deploying Pocket PC Setup Applications" at *http://msdn.microsoft.com/library/default.asp?url=/library/en-us/dnnetcomp/html/netcfdeployment.asp*.

Change the configuration of your Smartphone application from Debug mode to Release mode. Build the CAB file for your application by selecting the menu item Build → Build Cab File.

Locate the *BuildCab.bat* file in *C:\MySmartphoneApps\ SampleApp\obj\Release* and use Notepad to edit it.

Replace the *cabwiz.exe* with *cabwizSP.exe*:

```
"C:\Program Files\Windows CE Tools\wce420\SMARTPHONE 2003\
Tools\cabwizsp.exe" "C:
\MySmartphoneApps\SampleApp\obj\Release\SampleApp_SMP.inf"
/dest "C:\MySmartphoneApps\SampleApp\cab\Release" /err
CabWiz.SMP.log /cpu ARMV4 X86
```

Copy *vsd_setup.dll* from:

```
C:\Program Files\Microsoft Visual Studio .NET 2003\
CompactFrameworkSDK\v1.0.5000\Windows CE\wce400\x86
```

into the directory for the processor platform you are targeting—for example, ARM4:

```
C:\Program Files\Microsoft Visual Studio .NET 2003\
CompactFrameworkSDK\v1.0.5000\Windows CE\Smartphone\
wce400\armv4
```

Now, run the *BuildCab.bat* batch file.

You should be able to locate the two newly built CAB files in *C:\MySmartphoneApps\SampleApp\cab\Release* (see Figure 4-10).

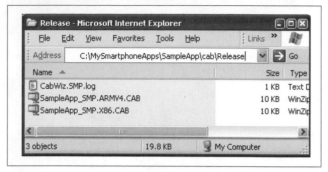

Figure 4-10. Locating the CAB files

Modify the *.inf* file to customize your installation (see Figure 4-11). Be sure to rebuild the CAB files if the contents of the *.inf* file have changed.

Create a simple HTML document and save it into your web server's root directory, such as *C:\inetpub\wwwroot*. Name the file *install.html*.

```html
<html>
<head><title>Download page</title></head>
<body>
  Download <a href="SampleApp_SMP.X86.CAB">
  SimpleApp</a>.
</body>
</html>
```

Copy the *SampleApp_SMP.X86.CAB* file into this same directory.

Launch Internet Explorer on the Smartphone and load the HTML document using *http://machine_name/install.html* (replace *machine_name* with the hostname or IP address of your server). You should see the screen shown in Figure 4-12.

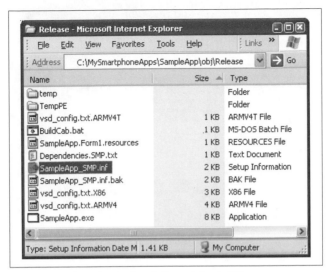

Figure 4-11. Locating the batch file and the .inf file

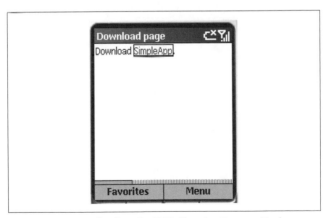

Figure 4-12. Downloading the CAB file using Internet Explorer on the Smartphone

Highlight the hyperlink and press the Action key. The CAB file will be downloaded and installed onto your Smartphone (see Figure 4-13).

Figure 4-13. Installing a Smartphone application

You can now locate your new application on the Start menu (see Figure 4-14).

Figure 4-14. Locating the installed application on the Start menu

Index

We'd like to hear your suggestions for improving our indexes. Send email to
index@oreilly.com.

For special offers from Microsoft associated with this book, please visit:
http://msdn.com/mobility

Microsoft®
.net Compact Framework